Kennan's Songs and Poems

Kennan Peacock

Presentation by *BookLeaf Publishing*

Web: www.bookleafpub.com

E-mail: info@bookleafpub.com

ISBN: 9789394788701

First edition 2022

LOVE LOVE LOVE LOVE

What do you love?

Is it your life or the stars up above?

Is it good? Will it grow?

Is it a thing you even know?

What is love and what's desire?

Are they both all-consuming fires?

Flesh and blood may lead astray but soul and
heart are forever the same

Like Rain

Soft like rain
Your mercy falls on me
One drop and I am saved
My elixir, my breathe of life
Your holy water rains gently
Singing me to sleep like a lullaby

Soft Like Rain

Magic rain
Sent from the heavens
Forms mud
God's grace
His Change

I melt, I think
Turn heat to vapor and vapor to heaven
From your steam, you rain down blessings

Your emotion, God
Like the ocean

What are you up to?

What are you up to?
What do you have in mind to do
today?

Will you give good advice or throw it away?

What are you up to?

Do you intend to be good?
Will you ever realize the flow of your mood?

Humanity Family

We all share the same blood
We all feel the same love

Why would we not live in harmony
If we are a part of one army

Marvelous Love, Marvelous light

Marvelous Love, Marvelous light

The stars they shine in the midst of night

The God above is watching over. He sees all
things, the smallest clover. The God of Earth is
with us still .He guards our planet and gives us
our fill

Word Power

Word Power

Your words hold a lot of power, they grow
stronger by the hour

Whether a tiny whisper or tasteful truth are
honored by your friends as solid truth

Be careful then to speak your mind and do it in
the nick of time

Tell your tale at the right moment and if you're
ready, be sure to own it

Magic Mind

Loose track of time
Stay a while in the pool
Of rhymes

Jive with the vibe

Squirrels

I will try to swallow my pride but please be with
me, let's unite

Brothers and sisters work together whether or
fare or foul be the weather

From sin or damage, you are made new
We all do as bad people do

We play, we fight, we argue, and quarrel
But let us learn to be like squirrels

They live in trees and goof around, they store up
nuts that fall to the ground
Then, when in the midst of winter, they fill their
bellies with a wonderful dinner!

Generations

Thankful for the generations
Who passed down loads of information
So we could down-load every sensation
Put what we don't have to imagination
Nothing can stop these vibrations
Our power and motivation
With love, comes the spring up of nations
Thank God, we will all roar like lions
Now that this world will one day
Belong to the multitude
An earth for everyone
Heaven on earth is yet to come
I won't be the only one to say thank you

Lingering Lust

12

I can still feel their every touch
I let my guard down, to show my love

Now the hands that run gentle fingers across my
hips and thighs
Are the dangling memories of three separate
guys

12

Self-Competition

I feel like a shallow breath
This life is all I have left
Lost great friends and admiration
Dreamt I could leave the nation
No disrespect
I love all my friends
Wish I could see everyone again
But not in my new sphere
What am I doing here

Like a shell this old body somehow still
resembles what I left behind
That perfect state of mind
Now replaced with an old soul
But you'd never know
Unless you looked deeper
At the lines and the wrinkles
Still breathing but barely
Not in the same way

I feel good about my poetry lately
Starting to act and sound
Like a lady
and I could almost be one
Here in the shallows of my room

Counting days to the next new moon
Feminine, divine keeping track of the time
Each day approaches, I get more
In tune with the ocean and the trees
Pollen won't make me sneeze

I'll sit and stand easily, with grace
This life ain't a race,
it's a self-competition

Choice

15

Listen to your heart, they say
But my heart has no mind
and my mind has no clue
And my soul won't choose

Bees, trees

Bees, trees
Bruises on my knees
To all these things I say, yes please

Shakespeare

17

Shakespeare tried but failed to sing
That would have been a wonderful thing

Imagine Shakespeare in his mind, singing songs
to pass the time

Mirror

I based myself in myself, not in God
I looked in the mirror and didn't know who I
was
I am who I am, I said
But who I am to be any better than dead
My heart cries out when there's peace & quiet
while the heart endures a trial of riot.
what I am in a mirror
Is just what I see
How could I be content with just a reflection of
me
It would be more thrilling and more of my type
to write out my insides
by pen or the type (writer)

Stubborn Love

All my love directed your way
I have feelings that I can't say

My eyes are wet from all these tears

My body's weak
I've skipped some meals

My mind's messed up
Nowhere to go

We felt so close but now we're both alone

Eternal Fight

21

With one breath we grow, the breath of God

Leading us from all that is odd. With hope and
without fear, we grow together
whether in fall, summer or in winter.

We can try to do what is right. Let us WIN this
eternal fight!

The Accidental Photo

The accidental photo
The image you create
With all the images
You never meant to take
The accidental photos
You find through your phone
That piece together an overarching tone
The hues, the colors, the life you see
The accidental photo
The understanding of your memories

The image you painted while asleep
The statue you sculpted by running in the mud
of the creek

The ancient ruins and arrowheads
Remind us of our remnants

Dusty, Rusty

Dusty, rusty, a little crusty
But the smell isn't so bad
In fact, I'm glad
Something about the dust smells like home
I'm not alone in these streets filled with my
neighbors, dead and alive
The dust doesn't irritate my nostrils,
It calms me
Like smoke to a bee hive
A smell reminiscent of good times

Life is feeling good again

Life is feeling good again
The sun is feeling warm again
My hands know how to touch again
I think I've caught the love again

Change the Tide

25

Let's change the tide, lose our pride. Life's a game if you're down for the ride.

Ain't it crazy how a woman loves her babies how two lovers make a child, how the truth is sweet and mild. But, only for a time. We like to repeat our own rhymes caught up in the motion of a disastrous love potion

We drown our thoughts in brandy, fill our guts with candy, drink water from an unclean well, fall into our people's spells

with all this commotion our minds are like oceans we rinse and repeat and we fall to our knees and the tears come and go but our thoughts we can't slow and our eyes do not follow because we feel incomplete; alone

yet, if we found a better way, a more eternal source to numb the pain

I speak of the light and the true we all know

Your heart and mind, they work together, we must learn to love one another.